500+ FUN Couples DATE NIGHT Ideas

Copyright © 2024 by Summer Valentine

All rights reserved.

No portion of this book may be reproduced, stored in a retrieval system, or transmitted in any form or by any means —electronic, mechanical, photocopy, recording, scanning or other—without written permission from the publisher or author, except as permitted by U.S. copyright law.

Published in the United States by Big Heart Books

*Dedicated to all the couples who
dare to keep the romance alive
and never stop having fun together:*

This book is for you.

Table of Contents

INTRODUCTION .... page 7

AROUND TOWN IDEAS .... page 11

ENTERTAINMENT IDEAS .... page 17

ATHLETIC IDEAS .... page 25

ADVENTURE IDEAS .... page 29

PLAYFUL IDEAS .... page 33

CRAFTY IDEAS .... page 39

ARTSY IDEAS .... page 45

BRAINY IDEAS .... page 51

AT HOME IDEAS .... page 55

CULINARY IDEAS .... page 63

ALCOHOL IDEAS .... page 71

NATURE IDEAS .... page 75

SEASONAL IDEAS . . . . page 81
LONG-DISTANCE IDEAS . . . . page 89

ADDITIONAL RESOURCES
Date Night Planning Tips . . . . page 93
Date Night Conversation Starters . . . . page 97
Your Turn! . . . . page 103

Introduction

Date nights are more than just a fun excuse to spend time together—they're an essential ingredient in maintaining a happy, healthy relationship. Research shows that couples who prioritize regular date nights tend to enjoy higher levels of satisfaction, intimacy, commitment, and communication.

Why are date nights so impactful? According to a report from the National Marriage Project and the Wheatley Institute titled *The Date Night Opportunity*, there are five key ways that date nights benefit and strengthen relationships:

Communication: Date nights provide a rare opportunity to connect and talk to each other about important topics without the distractions of work or family life getting in the way.

Novelty: Date nights are an opportunity to try new and exciting activities together that brings a fresh sense of adventure to the relationship.

Romance: Date nights support more romantic outings and connections as well as greater physical intimacy, which help sustain and deepen love.

Commitment: Dedicated one-on-one time reinforces a couple's sense of togetherness, strengthening their sense of commitment, which forms the foundation of any healthy relationship.

Stress relief: Stepping away from daily stressors to enjoy each other's company helps couples recharge and extend emotional support to one another.

Each of those elements adds up to fact that regular date nights are a small but powerful investment in any relationship: Whether it's reigniting the spark, discovering a shared passion, or simply enjoying quality time without distractions, the value of date nights cannot be overstated.

While you don't have to be a scientist to figure those things out, one powerful insight that scientists did discover from their research was that the sweet spot for reaping the benefits of date night is a lot more manageable than you might expect: about once a month.

Couples in the study who reported going on monthly date nights were the least likely to split up. Unfortunately, research has shown, time and again, many couples forgo this vital component entirely: Nearly half of all couples surveyed said they do not have a regular routine or frequency for engaging in date nights.

That's where this book comes into play. We've compiled more than 500 of the most memorable, amusing, and one-of-a-kind ideas that will make it easy for you to get excited about your next date night, ensuring that you put them on your calendar, month after month.

INTRODUCTION

And, don't worry, these ideas go beyond just dinner and a movie. You'll find ideas for nearly every interest and affinity out there, as well as some you probably never would have thought of! They are curated across more than a dozen themed lists, allowing you to find something that works for each you—even the men!

These ideas will help you experiment and try new pursuits while creating lasting (and maybe even some laughable!) memories together.

HOW TO USE THIS BOOK

Explore together: Dive into the lists to find ideas that suit your style and interests. Whether you're looking for something active, relaxing, creative, or adventurous, you'll find plenty of inspiration. Consider taking turns picking and planning date night so that you can tailor them to both of your personalities.

Consider all categories: Many ideas have crossover potential, however, for organizational purposes we've listed each one only once. For instance, "Eat a candlelit dinner," could have easily fit on the "At Home Ideas" list, but we've instead grouped it with "Culinary Ideas."

Mix and match: Feel free to combine ideas to craft the perfect date. For instance, perhaps you want to combine going horseback riding and watching the sunset together. Or, relaxing in the hot tub after having created your own signature drink. The possibilities are endless!

Track your adventures: Checkboxes are included with each date-night idea so you can mark off the dates you've tried, and pages are included at the back of the book for tracking new dates you try or brainstorming your own ideas.

Additional resources provided: In the back of the book, we've also included some additional resources to help you make your next date night a success with tips for taking a variety of constraints into consideration (children, budget, time, etc.) when planning your next date night, as well as a list of 50 conversation starters you can use on your next date night to connect on a deeper level.

So, grab your partner and start perusing our lists of ideas. From activities to games to new experiences and hobbies to try together, we've got tons of out-of-the-box ideas that will keep you busy and bonding, no matter what your interests or stage of life.

Get ready for your best date night ever—this is going to be fun!

Around Town Ideas

Buckle up and spend an evening exploring all that your town has to offer. Uncover the unique, unexpected, and delightful places within driving distance as you hit the road with one of these date-night ideas.

▪ **Recreate your first date.** Take a trip down memory lane by recreating your first date together. Wear similar outfits, get the same kind of meal, and revisit similar places. Reliving those first-date feelings can reignite the spark and remind you both of how it all began.

▪ **Plan a surprise adventure day.** Take turns planning a surprise outing or activity for your partner. It could be as simple as exploring a new part of town or visiting a quirky museum, but the element of surprise makes it special!

▪ **Do the alphabet date night challenge.** Choose a letter, like "S," and plan the whole date around it—start with a smoothie, then visit a sculpture garden, and end with stargazing. This creative twist adds to the fun as you brainstorm ideas corresponding with your chosen letter.

■ **Plan a "choose your own adventure" date.** Add an element of surprise by planning a date where you partner has multiple choices to pick from—but must select without knowing what they are! Once they make one choice, offer them another set; choices can be simple like choosing between two flavors at an ice-cream shop or deciding whether to turn right or left out of the restaurant.

■ **Create alternate personas for an evening out.** Have you ever wished you could be someone else? Well, here's a date-night to make that a reality: Dress the part, choose unique names, and invent backstories as you inject some playful drama into your evening.

■ **Dress each other up for the night.** Give each other full rein to your wardrobe and pick out date-night outfits for each other—no vetoes allowed! It's a fun exercise in embracing the unexpected as you don them out in public, even if it's just to the grocery store or a restaurant.

■ **Have a dollar store shopping challenge.** Here's an affordable scavenger hunt: Head to the store with a list of specific items you each must purchase for the other person within a set time and budget. Afterward, reveal your finds and see who came up with the best surprises. Here are some items you might want to include on your list:

- ☐ A favorite snack or candy
- ☐ A greeting card expressing how you really feel
- ☐ An inflatable balloon
- ☐ Ingredients to make dinner
- ☐ Something useful your partner needs
- ☐ Something your partner *must* try
- ☐ Something for you both to enjoy together

AROUND TOWN IDEAS

■ **Go on a secondhand treasure hunt.** Whether it's at a flea market, antique shop, or yard sale, see what hidden gems you unearth as you try to find quirky or meaningful items for each other that will double as unique keepsakes.

■ **Start a collection together.** Is there an object, animal or interest that is meaningful to you both? Why not start a collection devoted to it? Head to an antique store or flea market and start building your collection, whether it's ceramic figurines, unique coffee mugs or old records.

■ **Be a tourist in your own town.** Every town has multiple tourist attractions—have you experienced them all? Whether it's a popular museum, scenic park, or hidden gem, use a site like TripAdvisor and scout out some new ones to visit.

■ **Explore your town using public transport.** See your town from a new perspective by hopping on public transit and letting the route guide your day! Get off at different stops and see what new places you discover!

■ **Explore a nearby town.** Plan a mini getaway by exploring a town nearby. Wander its main streets, discover hidden gems, and dine somewhere new. It's a fun change of scenery and feels like a mini adventure without going too far from home.

■ **Go on a scavenger hunt.** DIY one with clues that lead you around your town and to favorite or memorable spots, or consider purchasing one through an app or local service so that you both can participate.

■ **Go on a geocaching adventure.** Geocaching takes you on a real-world treasure hunt, thanks to apps you can download that guide you to hidden containers or "caches" that others have left. Oftentimes, they're hidden in plain sight and the hide-and-seek element of it will help you work as a team to uncover each one!

▪ **Visit a weird or unique museum.** From niche topics (like rare minerals or the history of bones) to quirky collections (think antique toys or cat figurines), there's a museum for every interest, which can make for memorable outings. Check out atlasobscura.com for lists by state.

▪ **Visit the zoo.** They're not just for kids! Zoos offer the chance to connect with exotic animals through exhibits, presentations and some even offer behind-the-scenes tours or interactive opportunities exhibits like feeding the animals.

▪ **Go to a petting zoo.** Spending time with animals is known to lower stress levels and can be a much-needed mood-lifter after a hard week. Take turns feeding or petting animals at one of these hands-on petting zoos and make sure to take plenty of selfies!

▪ **Visit an aquarium.** Deep dive into the underwater world at an aquarium, which oftentimes also features touch tanks, where you can stroke a sting ray or pet a starfish. It will bring a real splash to your next date!

▪ **Get your pictures taken in a photobooth.** Check out local malls or search photobooth.net to find a photobooth near you. Then close the curtain behind you and say cheese on this classic date idea, sure to bring smiles!

▪ **Visit a pet store or animal rescue.** Head somewhere where you can play with kittens or pet the puppies together. It's helpful for the animals but also ultra-adorable for your relationship!

▪ **Go to a cat café.** Can you imagine a more purrfect date? Now available in many cities, they allow you to sip your favorite coffee or tea as you interact with playful, curious kitties.

▪ **Visit a local farmer's market together.** Stroll through a local farmer's market to discover fresh, seasonal produce, unique finds, and handmade goods. It's a relaxing way to explore your community and pick out ingredients for a homemade meal or dessert.

▪ **Attend a local festival.** Whether it's an event dedicated to music, food, a niche interest or a specific holiday, local festivals offer unique experiences to try something new while plugging into your community.

▪ **Book a couples' massage.** A couples' massage is a perfect way to relax and connect on a deeper level. You can book one at a spa for the ultimate pampering experience or try giving each other massages at home with oils, music, and soothing lighting.

▪ **Soak in a hot tub.** Even if you don't have a hot tub at home, many gyms, recreation centers or even hotels or rentals can provide access to a hot tub where you can soak up the good vibes together.

▪ **Try float therapy together.** Kick back and relax like never before in a float tank (also called a sensory deprivation tank). Offered at many wellness centers, they allow you to relax in saltwater while removing all sensory input for a mesmerizing and deeply calming experience.

▪ **Try out a sauna.** Sweat out the stress with a relaxing sauna date! You can find saunas at most gyms, wellness centers, and even some spas. This warm, steamy setting is perfect for reconnecting in a peaceful atmosphere while reaping a variety of health benefits.

▪ **Volunteer together.** Spend an evening giving back by volunteering together for a cause that's meaningful to you both. It could be helping at a local shelter, serving at a community kitchen, or cleaning up a park. It's a fulfilling way to bond and make a positive impact together.

▪ **Stay at a bed-and-breakfast.** These charming inns often offer unique, homey accommodations and (true to their name!) a delicious homemade breakfast. Think of it like a home away from home—without any of the chores or clean-up!

▪ **Rent electric scooters to tour your town.** Many towns offer scooters to rent, so why not spend an evening zipping around town on one? It will give you the chance to see your city (or a neighboring one) from a new perspective: Full speed, ahead!

▪ **Stay at an Airbnb.** Escape for the night by booking a nearby homestay. Whether it's a cozy cabin, a chic studio, or a quirky cottage, the change in surroundings can be a fun way to mix things up without having to travel far from home.

▪ **Rent a limousine for the night.** Whether you're heading to dinner, a concert, or just cruising around town, renting a limo will add a luxurious touch that will make you feel like VIPs.

Entertainment Ideas

Enjoy a night out filled with laughter, music, and unforgettable performances! Whether you're watching the action or joining in yourself, these ovation-worthy date ideas are all about letting loose and having fun.

- **Attend a murder mystery show.** Many venues host interactive dinners, complete with actors and hidden clues, where you can work together to solve a mystery. Enjoy the suspense, figure out the clues, and try to unmask the culprit before the night ends!

- **Attempt an escape room together.** These venues are an immersive experience where you use clues to solve puzzles so as to "escape" before time runs out. It's an invigorating challenge that will put your problem-solving skills to the test!

- **See a favorite band play.** Nothing beats the excitement of seeing a favorite band live! Enjoy the energy of the crowd as you sing along to your favorite songs together.

■ **Attend a music festival.** Spend an evening (or a weekend) at a music festival where you can rock out to a variety of performances, try festival foods, and dance the night away.

■ **Visit an amusement park together.** Live like a kid again at an amusement park! Ride roller coasters, play carnival games, and enjoy classic park treats like cotton candy and funnel cakes for a fun-filled day of thrills.

■ **See a demolition derby or monster truck rally.** For a date packed with high-octane action, check out one of these performances where cars crash, monster trucks jump, and engines roar.

■ **Attend a car or horse race together.** Pick your favorites to win, count down with the clock, and feel the rush as the racers cross the finish line for an adrenaline-packed experience.

■ **Attend a car show.** If you like a nice set of wheels, why not spend an evening at a car show? Whether they're antique, souped-up or luxury models, you'll get to be up-close-and-personal with one-of-a-kind automobiles, sure to rev your engines!

■ **Attend comic-con together.** Step into the world of superheroes, fantasy, and sci-fi by going to Comic-Con or a similar convention together where you can embrace your inner geek and even dress up in costume!

■ **Go to a state or county fair together.** Enjoy the classic charm of a state or county fair with rides, games and fried foods that can provide a nostalgic date you won't soon forget.

ENTERTAINMENT IDEAS

Go country line dancing. Dust off your boots and kick up your heels! Line dancing is easy to pick up, and the group energy is contagious as everyone dances along in unison to the same steps.

Ride an electronic bull. Saddle up and hang on for the ride of your life! See who can stay on the longest and have fun rooting each other on.

Visit a Renaissance faire or festival. Take a trip back in time to the world of knights and castles as you experience jousting, costumed performers, and medieval food. Dress up to make it even more fun!

See a roller derby. Roller derby is a thrilling sport to watch as skaters race, block, and score points in a fast-paced match that will provide a unique, action-packed date night.

Go to the circus. Experience the thrill of the circus for an evening filled with incredible stunts, acrobatics, and awe-inspiring performances. From tightrope walkers to jugglers, there's no shortage of wonder under the big top.

Go to a rodeo or tractor pull. Pull on a pair of boots and belt-buckle up as you cheer on modern-day cowboys as they ride horses, lasso bulls, or drive massive tractors for some down-home thrill.

Go to a comedy club. They say laughter's the best medicine, so prepare to laugh out loud until your cheeks hurt by seeing a stand-up comedian. With new acts and fresh material, every night at a comedy club brings something unexpected and hilarious.

▪ **Take an improv class together.** Think you're funny? Or wish you were funnier? Lighten things up by taking an improv class together, where you'll learn to deal with the unexpected, think on your feet, and laugh the night away!

▪ **Sing karaoke together.** Whether you're singing along at home with karaoke videos or at a karaoke bar, karaoke is a chance to let loose and have fun together, even if you sing a bit off-key!

▪ **Go to an open mic night.** Cheer on local talent as they share their music, poetry, or comedy on stage. Maybe even participate if you're brave enough!

▪ **Attend a live recording of a local television or radio show.** Local stations or shows sometimes offer these, whether as special events or routine occurrences. They will give you a behind-the-scenes glimpse as you watch the production unfold!

▪ **Ride a Ferris wheel.** Enjoy the view, hold hands, and take in the sights as you slowly rise to the tippy-top. It's an iconic date activity that's as charming today as it was on the first fairgrounds.

▪ **Ride a carousel.** Rekindle a sense of whimsy by riding a carousel together! Pick your favorite character, climb aboard and then enjoy the gentle up-and-down ride as you spin round and round.

▪ **Attend a live outdoor music performance.** Whether it's a jazz band in the park or an open-air concert, outdoor performances are sure to hit the right chord for a relaxed, music-filled evening together.

ENTERTAINMENT IDEAS

- **Apply to be on a reality show together.** Don't just watch your favorite reality show—try out for it, too! Take turns filming one another and submitting applications to be on a favorite show for the ultimate reality check!

- **See a movie in 3D.** Now offered in many theaters, 3D movies can be a way to supercharge an ordinary movie outing. Whether it's an action movie, nature documentary, or animated film, 3D technology offers a new perspective on your movie-going experience.

- **See an IMAX movie.** With larger-than-life screens and immersive surround sound, these special movies offer a one-of-a-kind cinematic experience. Found in many major cities, these theaters showcase movies filmed specifically for the format.

- **Visit a drive-in movie theater.** You'd be surprised how many of these nostalgic cinemas are still around. Search a database like DriveInMovie.com to find one nearby, pack some pillows and blankets and then cozy up with a movie under the stars!

- **Go to a dinner movie theater.** These theaters often have comfy seats, unique menus, and an immersive viewing experience that will give a new spin to the classic dinner-and-a-movie date night.

- **Set up a projector to watch a movie.** Bring the theater experience home by setting up a projector and watching a movie on a large outdoor or indoor screen.

- **Watch a black-and-white or silent movie.** Take a trip back in time as you enjoy the charm of old Hollywood.

Experiencing a vintage film makes for a unique, romantic evening.

▪ **Try a new movie genre.** If you think you've seen it all, step outside your cinematic comfort zones and check out a new movie genre. Whether you want to channel the serious, silly, scary or something in between, here are some suggestions for different genres to consider:

- ☐ Action films
- ☐ Epic adventure films
- ☐ Survival films
- ☐ Martial arts films
- ☐ Spy films
- ☐ Superhero films
- ☐ Science fiction
- ☐ Apocalyptic
- ☐ Space exploration
- ☐ Mysteries
- ☐ Psychological thrillers
- ☐ Horror films
- ☐ True crime stories
- ☐ Dramas
- ☐ Movies based on a book
- ☐ Biopics
- ☐ Historic movies
- ☐ Documentaries
- ☐ Comedies
- ☐ Romantic films
- ☐ Romcoms
- ☐ Dark comedies
- ☐ Musicals
- ☐ Animated films
- ☐ Indie films
- ☐ Film noir

ENTERTAINMENT IDEAS

- ☐ Cult classics
- ☐ Remakes & reboots
- ☐ International films
- ☐ Bollywood
- ☐ Anime

Athletic Ideas

Research shows that couples who share fitness activities are generally happier and healthier, so why not strengthen your bond as well as your muscles by incorporating some athletics into your next date night!

- **Participate in a 5K or marathon together.** Research a cause that matters to you both and get those endorphins running together. Maybe even make it more fun by dressing up in silly costumes when you hit the pavement!

- **Participate in a "color run" or "mud run" together.** If you're not afraid of getting messy, check out one of these races where you can get sprayed with colorful powders or crawl through the mud. It's a one-of-a-kind experience, and just think of the photos afterward!

- **Go bowling.** Bowling has long been a classic date night option for good reason: It's easy to pick up and accessible at almost any age. Some places even offer glow-in-the-dark bowling that can make even gutter-balls look cool!

■ **Play minigolf or go to the driving range.** Both are fun alternatives to the game of golf that almost anyone can play, whether it's trying to maneuver a golf ball through a fun maze of obstacles or seeing who can whack it the farthest.

■ **Go for a bike ride together.** Plan a scenic bike route, whether that's on a nature trail or even around the city. Either way, you'll feel super romantic with the wind blowing through your hair. Bonus points if you can rent a tandem bicycle and hum the lyrics to Nat King Cole's classic love song, "A Bicycle Built for Two" as you ride!

■ **Attend a sports game together.** Whether it's a professional, semi-professional or even just a local high-school team, it can be fun to sit in the stands together and root your team on to victory together.

■ **Go on a stadium tour.** For sports fans, a stadium tour is a unique date that lets you see behind-the-scenes of your favorite team's venue. Many stadiums offer tours where you can check out the locker rooms, stand on the field, and see areas usually only reserved for players.

■ **Go the batting cages.** Knock it out of the park with a date to the batting cages. Swing for the fences and see who can hit the most balls or whose hit flies the farthest.

■ **Go ice-skating.** Bundle up and glide hand-in-hand on this cozy winter date, perfect for keeping you both warm despite the chill.

■ **Take a fitness class together.** Whether it's spinning, kickboxing, or cardio, exercising together is a great way to

ATHLETIC IDEAS

bond while staying active. It's a surefire way to strengthen not only your body but your bond, too.

▪ **Try couples yoga together.** This is all about—literally—supporting each other as you move together in sync. Find guided videos or simply take turns trying different poses together.

▪ **Go swimming.** Whether you're at a pool, lake, or beach, a swimming date is both refreshing and fun. Maybe even bring some pool floats as you enjoy a playful day that's a real splash!

▪ **Go standup paddle boarding.** This activity combines the serenity of being on the water with a full-body balance workout that's both energizing and relaxing. Paddle side by side, enjoy the scenery, and cheer each other on as you find your footing navigating the inevitable ups and downs of this outdoor challenge!

▪ **Try a two-player sport.** Whether it's trying a new sport neither of you have played or reviving an old one from your peewee days, have a ball together! Here are some good sports to try that are perfect for two players:
- ☐ Tennis
- ☐ Squash
- ☐ Badminton
- ☐ Disc golf
- ☐ Ping pong
- ☐ Shuffleboard
- ☐ Handball (called singles)
- ☐ Padel

▪ **Learn a new dance.** Dance can be a great way to build intimacy between you and your partner as you work up a sweat, express some creativity and get in step together. Attend a class or watch a video to learn the steps to a new dance, such as:

- ☐ Salsa
- ☐ Samba
- ☐ Rumba
- ☐ Flamenco
- ☐ Tango
- ☐ Cha Cha
- ☐ Swing
- ☐ Ballroom
- ☐ Tap dancing
- ☐ Square dancing
- ☐ Country two-stepping
- ☐ Irish dancing
- ☐ Bollywood dancing
- ☐ Belly dancing
- ☐ Party dances (Macarena, Electric Slide, Hustle, etc.)
- ☐ Hip-hop
- ☐ Break dancing
- ☐ TikTok dance trends

Adventure Ideas

Turn your next date into an adventure you'll never forget! Whether you're conquering a new challenge or exploring uncharted territory, these ideas will get your hearts racing in the best way!

▪ **Take a helicopter tour or hot air balloon ride.** Soar to new heights when you take to the skies! Marvel at breathtaking views with one of these sky-high adventures!

▪ **Find a nearby ziplining course.** Fast track your next date night by zipping through the treetops together at an adrenaline-fueled zipline course. Many zipline parks offer varied heights and lengths of lines, so you can choose the right level of excitement for both of you.

▪ **Go to a smash or rage room.** They're all the rage for good reason: These rooms allow you to release pent-up stress by breaking objects in a controlled environment. For a date night, it can be cathartic getting to let off a little steam together and leave with a renewed sense of calm.

Explore a graveyard. Wander among the headstones, uncover pieces of local history, and be on the lookout for anything eerie during your visit. Many graveyards feature meandering walking paths and benches that can make for a serene—not to mention, spooky!—time.

Go ax-throwing. Ax-throwing venues have become popular attractions for a reason: They're exciting and surprisingly therapeutic. Learn the basics from an instructor, practice your aim, and challenge each other to see who gets the best score!

Explore with night-vision goggles. Available to rent from outdoor adventure companies or specialty stores, night-vision goggles will bring the wild world outside your backdoor to life like never before! Explore your neighborhood or a public park (make sure to check its hours) and see if you can spot nocturnal animals like owls, raccoons, or bats.

Take a lighted boat out on the water. Experience the magic of being on the water at night with an inflatable kayak or paddleboard equipped with underwater LED lights. These lights create an ethereal glow that illuminates the water and attracts curious fish. Be mindful of local regulations, as some parks and waterways may close after dark.

Go to the gun range. In a safe and controlled atmosphere, it can be fun to take your shot at the shooting range. Instructors can provide guidance and teach you proper technique, then you can aim, fire, and see how close you get to the bullseye!

ADVENTURE IDEAS

▪ **Try skeet shooting.** See if you're up to the mark by going clay target shooting, often available at outdoor ranges or shooting clubs. You'll use a shotgun to shoot clay discs that are launched into the air, giving you the satisfaction of shooting a moving target and seeing who's the better marksman.

▪ **Take an aerial arts fitness class.** These classes, often featuring silks, hoops, or trapeze, combine physical fitness with artistic expression, making them perfect for couples looking to elevate date night and grow stronger together.

▪ **Take a knife or sword fighting class.** Available at some martial arts gyms, these classes often cover the basics of weapon handling, footwork, and techniques for controlled sparring that'll have you both looking sharp!

▪ **Go metal-detecting.** Set off on a modern-day treasure hunt with a metal detector, which you can often rent from local hobby shops or find at sporting goods stores. Make it a competition to see who can find the most interesting item or set a fun goal like finding enough loose change for coffee afterward.

▪ **Go horseback riding.** Saddle up! Whether it's a guided trail ride through scenic countryside or a lesson at a local stable, this activity combines the thrill of the outdoors with the tranquility of connecting with nature—and each other.

▪ **Go mountain biking.** Explore the great outdoors by hitting a nearby trail on two wheels. Mountain biking together will give you a sense of adventure as you navigate rugged paths while basking in scenic views together.

▪ **Go indoor skydiving.** Enjoy the thrill of skydiving—without having to jump out of a plane! Indoor skydiving lets you experience the excitement of freefalling in a safe, controlled environment.

▪ **Go indoor rock climbing.** Whether you're beginners or pros, indoor climbing gyms offer a variety of climbing routes that can be a fun way to bond while pushing each other to new heights.

▪ **Play paintball.** Add some color to your date night with a high-energy date that will get your adrenaline pumping. It's a fun way to be active, strategize, and enjoy plenty of laughs (and maybe a few colorful battle scars) along the way.

Playful Ideas

They say that couples who laugh together, last together, and researchers have found that's true. So, play your cards right with one of these fun-filled ideas that are intended to be—quite literally!—a laughing matter.

- **Try the "don't laugh" challenge.** Tell the cheesiest jokes you can find while keeping a straight face and see who cracks first. It's sure to be a laugh a minute!

- **Play around on a playground.** Do you remember the last time you sped down the slide or spun on a merry go round? Rectify that by taking a trip to your local playground for an evening of child's play!

- **Attend a trivia game night.** Many bars and cafes host trivia events where you can answer questions on various topics. It's a lively and entertaining way to work together, strategize, and test how much you know as a team.

- **Play laser tag.** Team up or play against each other as you duck, dodge, and aim for victory. It's an active, playful way to spend time together and share a few laughs along the way.

▪ **Go to a pool hall.** Rack up a few games for a casual, laid-back date where you can keep your eye on the eight ball or play a game of darts together.

▪ **Play paint ball, DIY-style.** Fill balloons with fabric-safe paint, wear white shirts and head outside to play tag. Chase each other around and pop balloons on each other's shirts for a unique keepsake that's also your own wearable art!

▪ **Play minute-to-win-it games.** Usually silly to watch and play, these popular challenge-style games often involve little set-up and make for laughable memories together. A quick search online will unearth a trove of options.

▪ **Take a circus class together.** You could learn to juggle or tightrope or even fly on the trapeze together! Have fun stretching yourself (perhaps quite literally!) by taking a circus class together.

▪ **Have a Nerf gun fight.** Turn your home into a battlefield, complete with silly sneak attacks and barricades made of couch cushions. Keep track of how many hits you each get, perhaps even crowning one partner the winner!

▪ **Go to a virtual reality arcade.** Also known as VR, participants use special headsets that make the games come to life, whether it's hunting zombies or solving puzzles. Level up your date night and see how many points you can score!

PLAYFUL IDEAS

▪ **Learn a magic trick together.** Look up instructions or watch a tutorial, then practice until you've mastered it. Plus, you'll have a new party trick you can use to impress others afterward!

▪ **Learn to juggle or hula hoop.** Tap into your playful side by learning a skill like juggling or hula hooping. It's a fun and lighthearted challenge, plus it's a great way to improve coordination and have a few laughs along the way.

▪ **Play darts.** Challenge each other to a round of darts, whether at home or a local pub. Test your aim, set fun rewards for winning rounds, and see who can get closest to the bullseye.

▪ **Go go-kart racing.** See who has the best driving skills as you speed around a go-kart course. It's a great way to fulfill a need for speed and get your hearts racing together!

▪ **Play video games.** Whether you're into retro arcade games, cooperative adventures, or intense competitions, playing video games together can be a fun, immersive way to connect and unwind.

▪ **Go to an arcade.** Play classics like pinball, claw machines or Pac-Man, and see who comes out with the most tickets. Maybe you can even win a prize!

▪ **Play bingo.** Create your own bingo night at home, complete with homemade bingo cards, snacks, and little prizes! Pick a fun theme for a quirky night of friendly competition.

▪ **Fly kites on a windy day.** Pick out kites and see who can keep theirs in the sky longest. It's an upbeat, carefree activity that will get your date night off to a flying start!

▪ **Play board games.** Dust off an old board game or try a new one for some friendly competition. You can play at home or check out a game café and feel like a kid again. Consider one of the following board games that are great for two players:
- ☐ Chess
- ☐ Checkers
- ☐ Chinese checkers
- ☐ Backgammon
- ☐ Jenga
- ☐ Othello
- ☐ Guess Who?
- ☐ Battleship
- ☐ Scrabble
- ☐ Connect 4
- ☐ Yahtzee
- ☐ Blokus Duo
- ☐ Ticket to Ride
- ☐ Codenames: Duet
- ☐ Jaipur
- ☐ Patchwork
- ☐ The Fox in the Forest
- ☐ Hive
- ☐ Schotten Totten
- ☐ Raptor
- ☐ Lost Cities
- ☐ Stratego
- ☐ 7 Wonders Duel

▪ **Play two-player card games.** Ace date night with a simple deck of cards! There are dozens of games to choose from, so you're bound to find one that suits your style. Here are some suggestions (look up instructions, as some may involve special rules for playing with only two players):

- ☐ Poker
- ☐ Blackjack
- ☐ Slapjack
- ☐ Spades
- ☐ Gin Rummy
- ☐ Crazy Eights
- ☐ Double Solitaire
- ☐ War
- ☐ High or Lower
- ☐ Cribbage
- ☐ Dutch Blitz
- ☐ Speed
- ☐ Nerts (or Racing Demon)
- ☐ Kings in the Corner
- ☐ Egyptian Rat Screw
- ☐ Bura
- ☐ Spit
- ☐ Golf
- ☐ Trash
- ☐ Casino
- ☐ Pinochle
- ☐ Durak
- ☐ Sixty-Six
- ☐ Whist
- ☐ Tute

▪ **Play lawn games.** Perfect for your backyard or a local park, these classic games are easy to set up and make for

a charming outdoor activity. Some suggestions of two-player lawn games include:
- ☐ Cornhole
- ☐ Bocce ball
- ☐ Horseshoes
- ☐ Yard dominos
- ☐ Giant Jenga
- ☐ Ladder toss
- ☐ Croquet
- ☐ Lawn bowling
- ☐ Lawn darts

Crafty Ideas

Roll up your sleeves and get crafty together! From one-of-a-kind projects to hands-on keepsakes you'll cherish forever, these hands-on ideas offer something for every interest. (Plus, be sure to check out our sister list, Artsy Ideas on p. 45, for even more inspiration!)

▪ **Create your own pottery.** Many pottery studios allow you to throw clay on a wheel or simply paint pre-made pieces. Whether you're shaping your own mugs or glazing a bowl, it's a creative experience—with a memorable keepsake!—that lets you bond over something truly hands-on.

▪ **Recreate Pinterest fails.** You know those super crafty projects that look nothing like the pin? Embrace the failure by finding a project that seems overly ambitious and see how well your version fares—or flops. It's a low-stakes, high-laughter date that highlights the joy in trying something new.

▪ **Try tie dying.** Pick out a few plain T-shirts or tote bags, gather your dye, and experiment with different patterns and color combinations. The end result will be a vibrant reminder of your unique date!

▪ **Design your own matching T-shirts.** Show off your creative side by designing matching T-shirts using fabric markers, iron-on transfers, or uploading a design to a website that will print and mail it to you.

▪ **Create your own button pins.** Using a button maker, design your own wearable buttons reflecting shared interests, inside jokes, or compliments from one another. Designs can be hand-drawn, cut from magazines, or designed on a computer and printed out.

▪ **Decorate clothing with patches.** Personalize a jacket or bag with patches, easily purchased online or in craft stores. Pick ones that reflect your personalities, allowing you to literally wear your heart on your sleeve in style!

▪ **Knit your own beanies.** Knitting a beanie is beginner-friendly and only requires a few basic stitches, which you can learn from online tutorials or an instructional book. Hats off to a relaxing, crafty activity that can also be a real head-turner!

▪ **Make your own chakra bracelet.** Thought to help balance energy, chakra bracelets are more than just a fashion trend for men and women alike. String beads in different colors to represent different chakras and add accents like lava stones (which can be infused with essential oils) to personalize your creations.

CRAFTY IDEAS

▪ **Learn to make balloon animals.** Sometimes life can feel like a circus, so embrace it by learning to make balloon animals! Start with basic shapes and see which of you has the magic touch.

▪ **Make stained glass.** Kits are available at most hobby stores and provide all the materials and instructions needed to make your own colorful, light-catching art that you'll both enjoy reflecting back on!

▪ **Create a mosaic project.** Transform tiles or small pieces of glass and mirror into works of art whether you use a kit and create coasters or work together on a larger project like a tabletop.

▪ **Create mosaic art using painted beans.** This crafty trend involves painting beans in various colors and gluing them on a canvas or board to create unique, textured images. Simple landscapes or animals work well and arranging them can be a relaxing, meditative process.

▪ **Try hydro dipping.** Fill a bucket with water, use spray-paint to apply various colors to the top of the water, then dip an object (like a small vase or flowerpot) into the bucket. The paint will transfer to the object smoothly, creating a one-of-a-kind marbled effect.

▪ **Learn origami together.** From cranes to flowers to unique animals, origami is a relaxing, creative activity. Use books or online tutorials to guide you as you transform pieces of paper into unique, folded sculptures together.

▪ **Create collage-style artwork.** Remember Eric Carle's *The Very Hungry Caterpillar*? Simple shapes cut from colored tissue paper were layered together to create striking images. Channel this into a fun date, creating your own collaged animal or plant.

■ **Build a miniature room box together.** A room box is a scaled-down version of a real room, created in a box or even in something small like a metal Altoid tin. Work together or create your own world in miniature!

■ **Create something with a 3D printer.** More common than ever, 3D printers allow you to custom-make small items like keychains or figurines. Spend an evening designing items for each other and then watch them print, like magic! If you don't already own or have access to a 3D printer, they're also available to rent.

■ **Try leathercrafting or wood burning.** Kits are available with everything you need to personalize items like leather keychains or engrave wooden plaques—allowing you to really make a lasting impression!

■ **Build a model kit together.** Choose a model kit of a classic car, airplane, or ship and spend the evening building and painting it together. Not only is it a fun project, but you'll have a lasting reminder of the time spent crafting side-by-side.

■ **Make something with plaster of Paris.** Known as "plastercrafting," you can easily mix this up to craft a variety of items like small planters, candle holders, wall plaques, or decorative handprints.

■ **Try screen printing.** Use it to custom-make designs for T-shirts, tote bags, or pillowcases. DIY kits make it easy to try at home with the right setup, or you can join a local class to learn the process. It's a creative way to personalize items you use every day!

Try linocut printmaking. Maybe you remember this from elementary school, but this traditional printmaking technique can add artisan flair to a number of projects: Carve your design into a soft linoleum block (kits are available), roll it with ink, and then stamp your one-of-a-kind handiwork onto cards, posters, or fabric.

Try custom metal stamping. Design your own keychains, charms, or bracelets using metal stamping! Get a kit that includes a few small metal blanks, and personalize them with initials, a date, or favorite words for a memorable craft date with keepsakes to match.

Take a glassblowing class. It's a unique artisan hobby that's surprisingly more accessible than you might think! Find a glassblowing studio near you to create glass art, such as small ornaments to custom vases. It's an unforgettable date adventure you can literally raise a glass to.

Try bottle cutting. Transform empty glass wine or soda bottles by cutting them into useful and decorative items. You'll need a bottle-cutting tool to get started but from there, you can upcycle them into birdfeeders, candle holders, or vases.

Try resin crafting. Also known as "resin pouring," epoxy resin can be used to create glossy creations like keychains, paperweights, and trays. You can purchase beginner kits, molds and even glitter to create objects that look completely store-bought.

▪ **DIY a neon sign.** Crafting your own neon sign is surprisingly doable with DIY neon kits! Use flexible neon wire to form words, names, or fun shapes to hang up. Create a phrase that has meaning for both of you, or use your initials to brighten up a shared space.

▪ **Upcycle thrifted items.** Breathe new life into discarded items by upcycling them with some creativity and a little elbow grease. For instance, you could paint an old picture frame, distress a bookcase, or stencil a side table for a doable DIY.

Artsy Ideas

Get your creative juices flowing by injecting artistry into your date night! Whether it's marveling over masterpieces, releasing your inner artist, or dancing to new rhythms, take artistic license with one of these exquisite experiences.

- **Go to an art museum together.** There's usually some kind of art museum in every town, so take some time to check it out its exhibits. Share your impressions of the pieces, maybe find one that reminds you of each other, or just enjoy admiring each display.

- **Attend an art opening or gallery hop together.** These are usually well-attended events that can be fun to do together as you soak up the artistry in community.

- **Learn a new language together.** *Oh là là!* Have you ever wanted to learn how to speak a new language? Or maybe just whisper sweet nothings to your partner? Try learning some key words and phrases together, whether it's with a class, video, or translation dictionary.

▪ **See a local theater production.** Support local talent by attending a theater production in your area, even if it's just a community show or high school performance.

▪ **See a ballet or opera together.** Classic artforms like ballet and opera can make you feel like you're stepping back in time. Plus, they usually take place in a theater setting where you can dress up, making them feel especially fancy.

▪ **Attend a symphony or orchestra.** Indulge in a night of elegance by attending a symphony or orchestra performance. There's something magical about being surrounded by live classical arrangements, which are sure to be music to both your ears!

▪ **Visit an outdoor sculpture park.** Sculpture parks are unique art galleries set outdoors. Roam the grounds for a relaxed nature walk combined with a one-of-a-kind art experience.

▪ **Learn calligraphy and write each other letters.** Brush up on your penmanship by learning this artform. Then, write love letters or copy favorite love poems for some old-fashioned romance!

▪ **Go to a record or music store.** Spend an afternoon browsing through records or old CDs at a local music store. Look for old favorites, discover new artists, or even pick an album purely for its cover art.

▪ **Create street art—legally.** Some cities have designated spaces or public walls where artists can legally create graffiti, oftentimes referred to as "free walls" or "graffiti parks." Find one near you (make sure to check any rules and restrictions), bring some spray paint, and leave a mark all your own!

Go on a sketchpad date. Head out to a lively spot like a downtown square or farmer's market, armed with sketchpads and pencils. Sit side-by-side and sketch the various people, objects, and moments that catch your eye. You'll be amazed at how differently you both saw the same scene, making it a fun way to connect over your unique perspectives.

Draw portraits or create silhouettes of each other. Release your expectations and use this exercise as an opportunity to observe one another closely and create a memorable (and likely amusing!) keepsake in the process.

Paint favorite quotes. Choose meaningful words or phrases to paint on canvases. Whether they remind you of each other or are individual inspirations, it's a date night that will really motivate you both.

Recreate a famous masterpiece. Pick an iconic painting, like Van Gogh's *Starry Night*, and recreate it, whether with paint, colored pencils, or any other technique. You don't need to be professional artists; consider it an exercise in creativity as you interpret the piece together.

Paint a still life. Still-life painting encourages focus and detail, so set up easels side-by-side and paint a simple object, like a fruit bowl or a flower vase. Display your finished pieces as a reminder of your artistic evening.

Create paint-by-number artwork together. Can you color inside the lines? Then you can be your own

Rembrandt! Pick up paint-by-number kids and create your own artful masterpieces.

■ **Be like Bob Ross.** Channel your inner artist with a Bob Ross painting session at home! Follow along with a classic episode, complete with "happy little trees," and see what masterpieces you each create.

■ **Create mod art.** Try a pop art project or make abstract designs that express your personalities. You'll each walk away with a unique piece that captures the fun and creativity of the night.

■ **Create pour paint art.** This method requires minimal planning—just pick your favorite colors, pour them onto a canvas, and gently tilt. The colors will blend and swirl naturally, creating abstract, marbled effects unique to each piece.

■ **Paint with balloons.** Fill balloons with different colors of paint, then place them on a canvas and take turns popping them with a pushpin or dart. When the balloon bursts, the paint will spray across the canvas, creating a real bang!

■ **Create string paint art.** Surprisingly simple and accessible for all skill-levels, you use string or yarn dipped in acrylic paint and pull the paint-covered string across the canvas or paper, creating abstract designs from the vibrant lines. It's especially stunning on black paper, where colors pop dramatically.

■ **Get tattoos together.** Create art that lasts and get inked together! Decide whether you want to get matching tattoos, or each pick your own. It's a memorable and lasting way to symbolize your bond and support one another during the process!

▪ **Get cassettes and record a mixtape together.** Go retro and create your own mixtape cassette! Pick meaningful songs or the soundtrack for your next adventure. It's a classic way to share memories and enjoy a blast from the past together.

▪ **Take Polaroid photos together.** Grab a Polaroid camera, a fresh roll of film, and head to a favorite spot where you can capture the moment with the press of a button. You'll create instant keepsakes you can cherish and look back on anytime!

▪ **Try nighttime photography together.** Head out into the evening with a camera or smartphone and practice capturing the beauty of nighttime. Play with long exposures to photograph light trails, cityscapes, or the starry sky. For best results, find a spot away from city lights, bring a tripod for stable shots, and experiment with slow shutter speeds.

▪ **Take photos with a drone.** Get a new perspective by flying a drone, fixed with a camera, and taking aerial shots! Available to rent, you can use it to capture areas that are meaningful to you both or to get overhead shots of the two of you together!

▪ **Create a YouTube video together.** Spend an evening creating a video, whether it's filming a tutorial, vlogging about a recent experience, or just your conversation about a specific topic. Maybe you'll discover you enjoy it and start your own channel!

Stage your own photoshoot together. Choose a theme or location, coordinate outfits, and take turns being the photographer and model or use a wireless remote to photograph you together. Whether the photos are serious or silly, it will literally be memories in the making! Here are some classic poses or places you might want to take a shot at:

- In a sunflower field
- In front of colorful mural
- On a rowboat or canoe
- On a bridge
- On a vintage couch in a field
- At a carnival
- From behind while holding hands
- With the sunsetting in the background
- While snow is falling
- While giving each other a piggyback ride
- While spinning around together
- While giving a backwards hug
- While slow dancing
- Recreate Grant Wood's *American Gothic* painting featuring a straight-faced farmer with a pitchfork
- Recreate a classic album cover scene, like Abbey Road

Brainy Ideas

Boost your brain while you bond! Whether you're exploring a library, solving a tricky puzzle, or diving into a fascinating lecture, these date ideas offer the perfect mix of curiosity and connection.

▪ **Go to a book signing together.** Do you share a favorite author or genre? Then check out local bookstores or libraries for when authors come to town. You'll learn more about their processes and can get a copy signed for your personal library!

▪ **Visit a greenhouse or plant conservatory.** Plants are known to boost your mental health and reduce stress, which is what can make them perfect for your next date night! Plus, many conservatories feature exotic plants, flowers, and even butterfly gardens, making you feel like you've wandered into a lush wonderland.

▪ **Visit a planetarium.** Oftentimes found at museums and science centers, planetariums are a chance for you to enjoy the night sky together, even in the middle of the day! With lights dimmed and stars projected all around, planetariums offer a romantic setting and a chance to learn about constellations, planets, and galaxies.

Visit a historic landmark or monument. Learn about the history hidden right in your area by seeking out historic landmarks to explore! Oftentimes, historic plaques or even actors at special times will help recreate the events marked there. Search the National Historic Landmarks and National Register of Historic Places (both at nps.gov) to discover sites near you.

Visit a museum. Spend an afternoon at a museum where you can immerse yourselves in fascinating exhibits that bring subjects like history and science to life. Museums often have interactive elements and rotating displays, making each visit unique.

Visit an outdoor living museum. Also known as open-air museums, these collections oftentimes include restored buildings and costumed reenactors who bring history to life through their immersive, interactive experiences. From pioneer villages to colonial towns, enjoy stepping back into earlier eras together.

Attend a historic reenactment. Many hobby organizations or cities stage annual reenactments of significant battles or other historic events, the most popular being Civil War battles, which usually take place during the spring and summer months.

Go on a historic home or garden tour. Many beautifully preserved sites let you peek into the past with tours highlighting their architecture, decor, and gardens.

Guided tours often provide fascinating insights into local history and the lives of the people who once lived there.

Solve logic puzzles together. Work together as a team to crack logic puzzles, which you can find in activity books, apps, or even printable PDFs online. Keep your minds sharp, strengthen communication, and celebrate when you solve each one!

Put together a jigsaw puzzle. Jigsaw puzzles are a proven way to relax, improve your mood while also building problem-solving skills and memory. Choose a puzzle (or create your own!) with a meaningful image and connect as you put the pieces together.

Build a 3D puzzle. 3D puzzles provide a unique twist on the classic pastime. You can choose from famous landmarks, animals, or even fantasy castles and work together to bring your creation to life.

Complete a LEGO set. Did you know LEGO makes sets specifically for adults? From intricate architecture builds to nostalgic movie-themed sets, these challenging projects are an opportunity to—quite literally!—build more creativity into your relationship!

Go to a library or bookstore. Spend an afternoon exploring the shelves together at a library or bookstore. Make it a scavenger hunt by finding old favorites, like beloved childhood books or novels you've both read, and see what new gems you might bookmark.

Attend a lecture. Oftentimes offered at universities or libraries, attending a lecture together can be an enlightening experience where you can learn from an expert more about history, science, culture and more.

▪ **Go on a blanket-and-book date.** Head out to a scenic park, lay out a blanket and take turns reading out loud from a book together. It's a laidback, literary date that will get you both on the same page.

▪ **Try a science experiment.** Bring out your inner child as well as some educational fun by doing a science experiment together! From building a baking soda volcano to creating a soda geyser, it's a playful way to get to pretend to be a kid again—and maybe get a little messy, too!

▪ **Listen to a podcast together.** Have you been wanting to check out a popular podcast, but can't find the time? Turn it into a date night where you can curl up together and press play! True crime podcasts or comedic routines make popular choices.

▪ **Start a podcast together.** Choose a topic you both enjoy discussing and record your conversation about it. Ask each other questions, share your own experiences, and maybe even upload it for others to discover and enjoy!

At Home Ideas

Who says you need to go out to have a great date night? These low-cost ideas prove that with a little creativity, you can have one-of-a-kind quality time together from the comfort of your own home—without breaking the bank!

Take a pretend vacation! Pick somewhere you'd like to go, then put on a travel documentary about the destination and order takeout from a restaurant that offers that cuisine. It's a fun way to get a taste of somewhere new from the comfort of home.

Revisit your childhood. Take a trip down memory lane and "time travel" to an earlier era in your life. Cue up a favorite show from the time, make the snacks you loved back then, and settle in as you share your pasts with each other.

Reminisce over your relationship. For a romantic and nostalgic date night, go through old photos, revisit journals or diary entries, and recall the details that have helped shape your relationship since its earliest days.

Slow dance together. Put on a favorite song, turn down the lights, and slow dance in your living room, kitchen or even backyard for a romantic evening that's bound to sweep you off your feet.

Have your own at-home dance party. Take a spin around the kitchen or clear the living room floor for a makeshift dance party! Whether you're grooving to nostalgic hits or trying out new moves, an at-home dance party brings a ton of energy and laughter to date night.

Try making trick shots. Made popular on social media, these viral videos use ping pong balls, water bottles, basketballs, and other objects, to land elaborate trick shots, like landing a bottle flip onto a ledge. Take turns filming each other's attempts for an added challenge—and maybe even post your best success!

Do an at-home escape room. You can purchase a premade escape room kit or find free printable versions online. Work together to solve puzzles, decipher clues, and "escape" before time runs out. It's a perfect way to have fun testing your teamwork and problem-solving skills from the comfort of home.

Play truth or dare. Rediscover this classic game with a date-night twist! Discover more about each other with deep questions or just have fun tackling playful challenges.

Build a blanket fort. Relive your childhood by building a fort. It can be as simple or as elaborate as your imaginations desire. Then, once it's finished, snuggle up inside where you can play games, watch a movie, or even enjoy a fancy, grown-up drink.

▪ **Have an indoor picnic.** Lay out a blanket on the living room floor, add some candles, and serve up simple snacks and appetizers. It's a cute, low-stress date night that feels like a treat without leaving the house.

▪ **Have a sleepover.** Wear matching pajamas, watch a movie, and maybe even have a pillow fight in this childhood throwback! Perfect for a cozy night in, it's a lighthearted way to let loose together.

▪ **Tell ghost stories in the dark.** Dim the lights, grab a flashlight, or gather around the fireplace and see who can share the spookiest (or silliest!) ghost stories.

▪ **Relax in a bubble bath together.** Soak, unwind, and connect by drawing a bubble bath for two. Add candles, a favorite scent, or some bath salts to transform your bathroom into a relaxing, spa-like setting without leaving home.

▪ **Give each other foot rubs.** Take turns giving each other foot rubs for an intimate and low-key way to connect, especially after a long week. Set up a cozy space with lotion, essential oils, or a foot soak as you pamper each other.

▪ **Snuggle under a blanket in front of a fireplace.** Baby, it's cold outside, so cuddle up under a cozy blanket in front of a fireplace! (You can always stream a virtual fire on your TV for a similar ambiance.) It's a simple, romantic way to unwind and see where the conversation takes you.

▪ **Do face masks at home.** Complete with cucumber slices on your eyes and a refreshing drink in hand, it's a simple date night that will leave you both glowing! (Don't forget to snap photos for a silly reminder!)

▪ **Try to meditate together.** While meditation is usually thought of as a solo endeavor, it doesn't have to be! Choose a guided meditation, dim the lights, and relax side by side as you soak up the mental and physical benefits of mindfulness.

▪ **Find out your love language.** Discovering your love languages can help you understand each other's unique ways of giving and receiving love. Take a quiz together, discuss your results, and talk about specific ways you can show each other you care with those insights in mind.

▪ **Take personality tests.** Learn more about each other by taking personality tests together. Whether it's the Myers-Briggs Type Indicator, DISC, or a fun quiz online, the results can spark interesting conversations and reveal traits you may not have known. Plus, it's a fun way to see how similar (or different) the two of you really are!

▪ **Learn hypnosis.** Hypnosis can be used to induce deep calm and relaxation for an unusual but soothing date night. Use an online tutorial or app for self-hypnosis or to learn how to hypnotize each other, and maybe even try incorporating lighthearted suggestions for each other!

▪ **Analyze each other's handwriting.** Tap into your inner graphologist by analyzing each other's handwriting. Whether you use an online guide or instructional book, it can be amusing to see what insights your handwriting might have to say about your personality.

AT HOME IDEAS

▪ **Find out each of your Enneagram types.** The Enneagram is an insightful personality system that dives into your core motivations and fears. Taking the test together can be a meaningful way to understand each other on a deeper level.

▪ **Read each other's tea leaves.** Steep some loose-leaf tea and then channel your inner mystic by trying to read each other's leaves left in the bottom of the cup. This age-old tradition, also known as tasseography, is a playful way to make predictions.

▪ **Read your fingerprints.** Try reading each other's fingerprints, an activity inspired by palmistry. Look up common fingerprint patterns like loops, whorls, and arches, and discuss what each one is said to reveal. It's a lighthearted, hands-on way to explore each other's unique marks.

▪ **Create a photo calendar.** Take an evening to go through your favorite photos from the past year together and upload them to create a custom calendar. It'll be like a walk down memory lane that will last all year long!

▪ **Write thank you notes together.** Make an evening of pinpointing people in your life you'd like to thank, whether for big things down to even the smallest gesture. Researchers have found the process immediately increases happiness—something you can both feel good about!

▪ **Create blessing bags to give out to people in need.** Pay it forward by filling small bags with essentials like toiletries, snacks, socks, and water bottles for people in need. Then, distribute them on your next date-night!

■ **Paint and hide kindness rocks.** Spread some kindness by transforming ordinary stones into one-of-a-kind "kindness rocks" with encouraging messages or uplifting scenes painted on them. Then, hide them around town for others to find!

■ **Create a time capsule together.** Great for an anniversary, gather meaningful items and write letters to each other for a time capsule you can open together in the future. Seal it up with a "do not open until" date and bury it or store it somewhere safe until then.

■ **Create a couples bucket list.** Sit down together and brainstorm all the things you want to do together. From dream vacations to small, everyday adventures, it's a great way to help each other achieve the goals that matter most. (If you need ideas, check out our sister book, *1000+ of the Best Bucket List Ideas*.)

■ **Live out a childhood dream together.** What's something you always wanted to do as a kid, but never got to? Work together to figure out some of those long-lost dreams and come up with a plan to make them reality together!

■ **Create "love maps" of each other.** This concept was developed by relationship expert Dr. John Gottman and involves developing intimacy with your partner by understanding each other's hopes, dreams, fears, values, and more. Search online for questions to help you build these love maps together.

■ **Do a sensate focus exercise.** This guided practice, often used in relationship therapy, helps couples explore touch and sensation together without the pressure of performance or expectations. Find instructions online for this unique bonding experience.

Try a bedroom roleplay. From pretending to be strangers at a bar to the classic doctor-and-nurse scenario, have fun bringing a roleplay fantasy to life by discussing and choosing one that appeals to each of you and playfully incorporating costumes and props.

Stage a boudoir photoshoot together. Try a sensual at-home photo session where you take turns photographing each other. Keep it private, have fun with poses, and focus on highlighting your intimate connection as a couple.

Create a "Yes / No / Maybe" intimacy checklist. Take some time to individually create a list of things in the bedroom that you would be open to trying, are unsure about, or are excited about. Compare your lists to find new ways to connect, as well as facilitate honest communication and deeper intimacy.

Do a body drawing activity. Use body-safe markers or paint to write notes on one another about your favorite body parts and why. This is a body-positive activity intended to highlight your attraction to each other, imperfections and all.

Dream about the future together. Take some time to talk about your goals and dreams for the future, both as individuals and as a couple. Perhaps even write emails to your future selves and schedule them to send on a future date using tools available in many email providers.

Culinary Ideas

Savor your time together with a foodie-favorite date! From whipping up a recipe together in your own kitchen to savoring delicacies out on the town, these ideas will fill not only your stomach but also your heart!

▪ **Eat a candlelit dinner.** Eating by candlelight creates an intimate setting that adds magic to even a simple meal making the experience feel special and memorable. Add soft background music and watch the sparks fly!

▪ **Enjoy breakfast in bed.** There's something luxurious about eating in bed, even if it's at night. Prepare ahead of time with takeout pastries or a programmed coffeemaker and then leisurely enjoy breakfast-for-dinner together.

▪ **Host your own cooking challenge.** Channel your inner chefs with a *Chopped*-inspired cooking challenge where you select random ingredients, set a timer, and see what creative dishes you each cook up. And if things go wrong? There's always takeout!

▪ **Try a taste-test challenge.** Surprise your partner by creating your own blind taste test and seeing if they can guess each item! Whether you use candy, soda, snacks, or another favorite treat, prepare a variety of samples, blindfold your partner, and have fun guiding them through the taste test.

▪ **Try a blind-baking challenge.** Mix together equal parts fun and flirting in this date-night challenge. Blindfold one partner while the other gives instructions, guiding them through a selected recipe. It's a sweet way to turn up the heat in the kitchen!

▪ **Recreate your favorite restaurant meal.** Find a copycat recipe online for a favorite restaurant meal to cook together at home. From saving some cash to savoring your homemade meal together, it's sure to be a recipe for success!

▪ **Take a cooking or baking class together.** Whether taking an official class or just watching a video online, learning to cook together can help you expand your horizons, work together as team, and then relish your culinary creations together!

▪ **Learn how to make something from scratch.** While most of our food and drink come from a grocery-store shelf, it can be fun to try making it yourself and learning how much work goes into that store-bought staple! Consider trying to make one of the following from scratch:
- ☐ Bread
- ☐ Pasta
- ☐ Ice cream

CULINARY IDEAS

- ☐ Cake pops
- ☐ Sausages
- ☐ Pie
- ☐ Pudding
- ☐ Jam or jelly
- ☐ Butter
- ☐ Pizza
- ☐ Pickles
- ☐ Granola
- ☐ Donuts
- ☐ Cinnamon rolls
- ☐ Tortillas
- ☐ Salsa
- ☐ Sushi
- ☐ Lemonade
- ☐ Apple sauce
- ☐ Vanilla extract
- ☐ Sweet tea
- ☐ Hummus

Make fondue. Have fun with fondue! Decide whether to use melted cheese or chocolate. Then dip an assortment of goodies like bread, fruit, or marshmallows in it for a fun, at-home treat.

Set up an ice cream sundae bar. Satisfy your sweet tooth together by going all out for an ice cream: Gather a variety of toppings and build to your hearts' content. Don't forget the cherry on top!

Share a bowl of spaghetti. Get cozy and serve up a big bowl of spaghetti to share, à la *Lady and the Tramp*. Take turns twisting the noodles, and maybe even recreate that iconic (if not messy!) kiss.

▪ **Build your own pizza night.** Turn your kitchen into a pizzeria and make DIY pizzas together. Choose your favorite toppings, experiment with combinations, and bake them just the way you like.

▪ **Cook a meal using aphrodisiac ingredients.** Honey, chocolate, strawberries, asparagus, pomegranate, figs, and oysters are believed to enhance libido, so whip up a meal incorporating some of them—and put their powers to the test!

Grill out at a park. Enjoy the relaxed atmosphere, cook up your favorite picnic dishes, and eat al fresco. It's a casual, delicious way to enjoy good atmosphere, good food, and each other's company.

▪ **Dine al fresco.** Take your meal outdoors and enjoy dining in the fresh air. Whether it's at a fancy restaurant with outdoor seating, a cozy patio, or even your backyard, it will literally be a breath of fresh air!

▪ **Do your own local food tour.** Pick a favorite food—like tacos, donuts, or ice cream—and scout out multiple eateries to order different varieties. Rank each stop based on things like taste, presentation, and atmosphere, and you'll have a memorable (not to mention yummy!) foodie adventure under your belts.

▪ **Eat at a fancy restaurant.** Are there any Michelin-rated restaurants near you? See what all the fuss is about and check out one of these luxury eateries. Dress up, savor unique dishes, and enjoy the sumptuous experience!

▪ **Eat at a food truck.** Whether you're trying tacos, noodles, or unique fusion dishes, food trucks are a low-key, delicious option that have become trendy, thanks to their convenience, affordability, and unique food offerings. Make it a food truck crawl and try a few for the ultimate street-food experience.

Go shopping at an ethnic grocery store. Feel like you've travelled the world by journeying to an ethnic grocery store and explore its unique offerings. Challenge yourselves to create a meal at home with what you find: a main dish, specialty drinks, and dessert.

Try samples at a grocery store. If you're in a mealtime rut or just want to try something new without much commitment, samples can be a fun (not to mention, free!) way to spend an evening. Grocery store chains including Costco, Sam's Club, Publix, Whole Foods, and Trader Joe's frequently offer bitesize samples you can munch.

Eat at a tapas restaurant. A tapas bar serves small plates of food, called tapas, which comes from the Spanish word that means "to cover." Order multiple small plates to share as you experiment and discover new flavors together.

Visit an ice cream parlor. This date is a classic for a reason: What's sweeter than a bowl of your favorite frozen dessert?! Sample unique flavors, grab a sundae to share, or try making your own combo as you treat yourselves!

Go to a coffee shop. Make a coffee date special by picking a cozy spot to relax together. Enjoy specialty brews, people-watch, or bring along a book to read side by side as you savor a cup of joe.

▪ **Try a new restaurant.** Bring a sense of adventure to dinner by trying a restaurant with a cuisine that's new to both of you! Many will also offer a unique ambiance as well, which will make this simple outing feel like a getaway. Consider one of the following cuisines:
- ☐ Mexican
- ☐ Caribbean
- ☐ Cuban
- ☐ Cajun
- ☐ Brazilian
- ☐ Venezuelan
- ☐ Spanish
- ☐ French
- ☐ Italian
- ☐ Greek
- ☐ Mediterranean
- ☐ Middle Eastern
- ☐ Turkish
- ☐ African
- ☐ Ethiopian
- ☐ Indian
- ☐ Himalayan/Nepalese
- ☐ Korean
- ☐ Thai
- ☐ Filipino
- ☐ Japanese
- ☐ Chinese
- ☐ Vietnamese
- ☐ Farm-to-table
- ☐ Breakfast
- ☐ Barbeque

▪ **Attend a food or drink tasting together.** They say the way to a person's heart is through their stomach, so

CULINARY IDEAS

why not try a tasting? Tastings often include informational presentations while you discover new favorites together. Consider finding a tasting for one of the following:

- ☐ Hot sauce
- ☐ Honey
- ☐ Olive oil and vinegar
- ☐ Cheese
- ☐ Ice-cream
- ☐ Chocolate
- ☐ Coffee
- ☐ Tea

Alcohol Ideas

Raise your spirits with a date you both can toast to! Enjoy responsibly as you sip, mix, or sample your way through an evening where the good times flow.

▪ **Go to a rooftop bar.** Take date night to new heights with a rooftop bar experience! Enjoy a drink, light bites, and panoramic views of the city. It's a great way to unwind while also enjoying the sunset or stars overhead.

▪ **Take a brewery tour.** For beer enthusiasts, a brewery tour will take you behind the scenes of how your favorite beer is made. Plus, many end with a tasting session, where you can try unique brews and learn about the flavors that make each one different.

▪ **Create your own signature drink.** Start by choosing your base—rum, gin, whiskey, or non-alcoholic options—then experiment with mixers, fruits, and garnishes. Give your drink a fun name and write down the recipe so you can make it for future celebrations together.

▪ **Create flaming drinks.** Fire up your next date night by making flaming cocktails. Look up a recipe like a "Blue Blazer" or a "Flaming Lamborghini" to try. (Ensure safety by using heat-safe glasses and working in a fire-safe area.)

▪ **Try a classic cocktail recipe.** Step back into an earlier era by mixing up a classic cocktail like a Manhattan, Sidecar, or Old Fashioned. You can even dress the part in vintage-inspired outfits and play era-appropriate music while you sip and imagine the good ole days.

▪ **Attend a drink tasting.** Many wineries, breweries or even specialty restaurants offer alcohol tastings so that you can sample different varieties and maybe find a new favorite. Here are some examples of alcohol tastings you might try to find:
- ☐ Wine
- ☐ Beer
- ☐ Whiskey
- ☐ Bourbon
- ☐ Gin
- ☐ Vodka
- ☐ Sake
- ☐ Cider

▪ **Take a mixology class.** Become your own bartender by taking a class, often offered at bars, community centers, or large liquor stores. You'll learn techniques like muddling, shaking, and garnishing, all while sampling new flavors and learning new skills you can use to shake up future date nights!

▪ **Go to a hookah lounge.** For a relaxed, low-key date, visit a hookah lounge where of-age patrons can try shisha, a special kind of tobacco that comes in a variety of flavors

ALCOHOL IDEAS

that is smoked through a water pipe. Many lounges feature cozy seating and dim lighting with ambient music for a relaxing evening.

Nature Ideas

Branch out and explore the wilderness right around you. Whether it's in your own backyard or in a nearby park or nature preserve, researchers have found that being outside offers tons of benefits to your wellbeing, which are only amplified when you share them with your special someone!

- **Plant a garden together.** Root for each other by planting a garden together! Select seedlings (perhaps choose ones you can use to create a dish you both enjoy, like basil and tomatoes for pizza or cilantro and peppers for fajitas) and then tend them together until they're ready to harvest!

- **Forage for mushrooms or other wild edibles.** Foraging for native edibles is a lost art—but it doesn't have to be! Head out to a nature preserve with a knowledgeable guide to find wild edibles growing naturally where you live. Afterward, use them to make a meal for an, ahem, un-spore-gettable date!

▪ **Go fruit picking.** Take a trip to a nearby orchard or fruit farm and enjoy a "berry good" day of fruit picking. Savor your seasonal harvest by cooking up a tasty dessert afterward at home.

▪ **Pitch a tent and sleep outside.** Set up a tent, cozy up with blankets, and spend a night under the stars together. Whether it's in your backyard or at a nearby campground, camping is a fun way to disconnect from everyday life and enjoy each other's company.

▪ **Plan an outdoor picnic.** Spice up your usual dinner routine by putting it in a basket, finding a scenic spot and lounging on a blanket while you eat. Fresh air, good food, and time to reconnect—it's the recipe for a perfect date.

▪ **Go on a nature hike.** Enjoy the great outdoors while you unplug from daily life and reconnect together on a nature hike! Search a site like alltrails.com to find nearby trails to explore.

▪ **Go bird watching.** Grab some binoculars, a guidebook or a bird identification app, and see how many species you can spot. Some parks even host groups where seasoned birders can help you get started. It might sound like it's for the birds, but don't chicken out on trying this surprisingly invigorating activity!

▪ **Go fishing together.** Fishing can be a relaxing way to unwind together. Plus, see who reels in the most fish—you might be surprised!

▪ **Go fly fishing.** Using a special fly rod and often done in streams or rivers, it's more of a challenge than typical fishing that makes for a slow-paced and rewarding way to bond, whether you catch anything or not.

Go canoeing, kayaking, or rent a paddleboat. Escape from the distractions of everyday life by hopping on a boat and exploring a local lake, creek, or river together. Enjoy the tranquility of the water as you connect with one another and nature, too!

Drive a scenic route. Did you know the U.S. Department of Transportation recognizes roads with notable scenic, cultural, history, natural or archaeological features as "scenic byways"? Find one near you (check out scenic.org for lists by state), pack a bag with snacks and turn a simple drive into a memorable adventure.

Visit a botanical garden. Botanical gardens can be like a setting out of a storybook, allowing you to take a romantic stroll through lush gardens where you can—literally—stop and smell the roses.

Visit an arboretum. An arboretum is a botanical garden specializing in trees and oftentimes features tranquil paths you can stroll and are especially beautiful in spring and fall when colors are at their peak.

Watch the sunrise. Start your day with a bit of magic by watching the sunrise. Bring along coffee or breakfast to enjoy as you watch the world wake up.

Watch the sunset. Head to a scenic spot, grab a blanket, and watch the sunset together. It's a simple yet stunning way to enjoy each other's company while nature puts on a show.

Stargaze at night. Head outside on a clear night with a blanket and a stargazing app like SkyView to help you identify stars and planets. Take turns finding constellations and learning the myths behind them, or make a wish on a shooting star. Bonus points if you bring a telescope!

Visit a local creek or lake. Roll up your pants and get your feet wet at a nearby waterway. You can skip rocks, look for crawdads, go fishing, or enjoy a picnic by the water's edge. The natural setting, along with the calming sound of flowing water, is sure to make a splash!

Join a guided nature walk. Check out your nearby county, state, or national park to see if they offer guided nature walks. Led by an expert, they're a great way to learn more about local flora, fauna, and ecology.

Learn outdoor survival skills. Sign up for a class on outdoor survival skills and learn things like how to build a fire or identify edible plants. It's both practical and exciting, and you'll gain new knowledge together that could come in handy for future outdoor adventures.

Feed the ducks at a local park. Grab a bag of duck-safe snacks (like oats or seeds) and head to a local pond or park for an outing that's just ducky!

Stay overnight at a farm. Called a "farm stay" or "agritourism," these mom-and-pop establishments are more common than you might realize and offer an opportunity to get up-close-and-personal with homegrown food and animals. Some include meals or even the chance to do farm work!

NATURE IDEAS

▪ **Take a boat tour.** Hop on a boat tour for a relaxing date on the water. Many cities offer scenic river or harbor cruises with unique views and often a bit of local history.

▪ **Watch a meteor shower.** Meteor showers happen year-round and are great opportunities to cozy up and try to spot a shooting star! The most popular annual meteor shower (the Perseids) peaks during August. Don't forget to make a wish!

▪ **Sit around a fire pit or fireplace.** Snuggle up together and enjoy each other's company in front of a crackling fire. Don't forget to bring marshmallows to roast!

▪ **Find and polish your own gemstones.** Find a creek, river, or gravel pit when you can sift through pebbles for unique stones. Then, polish your finds at home with a rock tumbler—perfect for hands-on nature lovers who want a small keepsake.

▪ **Enjoy a thunderstorm together.** There's no reason that a thunderstorm has to ruin date night. Instead, turn it into a date of its own! Set up a cozy, covered spot and watch as lightning fills the sky. You could even try using a camera to capture lightning photography or read folktales about lightning.

▪ **Relax in hammocks.** Known as "hammocking" or "mocking," this activity involves tying a hammock between two trees or poles (positioned about 10 feet apart) in a local park. Then, you literally "hang out" together—relaxing, swinging or even taking naps as you soak up the great outdoors.

▪ **Pick up litter together.** It's a feel-good activity that lets you work as a team and enjoy the outdoors while making a positive impact. Grab gloves, trash bags, and choose a park or roadside to clean up. Reward yourselves afterward for your good deed!

Seasonal Ideas

Make the most of every holiday and season with these themed date ideas. From cozy winter nights to splashy, summertime celebrations, these festive dates will help you make the most of each passing season.

▪ **Eat a traditional New Year's Day meal.** It's a Southern tradition to ring in the New Year with a hearty meal of black-eyed peas, which is said to bring good luck and prosperity in the year to come.

▪ **Play in the snow together.** When the snow falls, bundle up and head outside for some winter fun! Have a playful snowball fight, make snow angels, or build a snowman together before heading inside to warm up together.

▪ **Go sledding or snow tubing together.** Pick a favorite snowy spot, bring a thermos of hot cocoa, and enjoy the thrill of speeding downhill together. It's a perfect winter date for adding some adrenaline (and laughter) to the season.

☐ **Go for a winter hike.** Embrace the quiet beauty of winter on a hike through snowy trails. With crisp air, sparkling snow, and tranquil landscapes, it's an invigorating way to enjoy the winter wonderland.

☐ **Taste test Valentine's Day chocolates.** Gather the season's best treats for a sweet taste test. From classic chocolate hearts to uniquely flavored gourmet varieties, see if you can guess them correctly or create a ratings card to track your favorites!

☐ **Cook an Irish dinner.** Whether it's a shepherd's pie, Irish stew, or Irish soda bread, celebrate St. Patrick's Day with a taste of Ireland! Play Irish music in the background and maybe even add a couple of drops of green food coloring to a light-colored drink (try ginger ale or beer).

☐ **Dye Easter eggs together.** Dyeing Easter eggs isn't just for kids; try new patterns, use natural dyes, or go for an artistic theme. It's an egg-cellent way to be creative while also getting festive!

☐ **Create an Easter egg hunt.** Surprise each other by filling eggs with treats, notes or playful surprises, and hiding them in separate rooms. Then guide each other to find them all for an egg-citing, grown-up Easter egg hunt for two!

☐ **Create a jelly-bean taste challenge.** Divide jellybeans of various flavors into two bowls, blindfold one partner, and see if they can identify each flavor before switching roles. Up the ante by mixing in unpleasant flavors, which you can find in specialty "bean boozled" packs.

SEASONAL IDEAS

■ **Play Easter egg darts.** Come out of your shell with this hilariously messy twist on the classic game of darts: Set up a target in your backyard and take turns throwing raw eggs at the bullseye, a task that's sure to crack both you up!

■ **Have a water fight.** Arm yourselves with squirt guns or water balloons and head to the backyard or park. For an extra splash of fun, consider adding fabric-safe paint to the water and wearing plain T-shirts so that each hit leaves a colorful mark!

■ **Blow up a backyard swimming pool.** Treat yourself to a mini vacation! Blow up a backyard pool, grab some towels, and mix up fancy drinks to sip to turn your backyard into a laid-back oasis for two.

■ **Watch Fourth of July fireworks together.** As the sky lights up with color, it's the perfect setting to cuddle up, enjoy the show, and maybe even make some of your own fireworks!

■ **Create a couples costume for Halloween.** Get creative together by planning a couples costume for Halloween! Pick a fun or quirky theme, gather the materials, and enjoy the creative process, no matter whether you wear them for a party, passing out candy, or just for photos.

■ **Take a ghost tour.** Lots of towns host ghost tours, especially around Halloween. Book one for a special, spooky date night!

▪ **Go to a haunted house.** Whether you laugh or scream together, it's a great bonding experience filled with excitement and adrenaline.

▪ **Find a corn maze.** Get lost together—literally!—on this fun fall date. Most corn mazes provide a map; use it and see if you can find your way out together.

▪ **Go to a pumpkin patch.** Nothing says fall like a trip to a pumpkin patch. Stroll through rows of pumpkins, take a hayride, and take photos together for a fun autumn outing.

▪ **Carve pumpkins together.** Pick out pumpkins, grab carving tools, and come up with unique designs together. Light them up afterward to see your handiwork glow, and you'll have custom-made decorations for Halloween.

▪ **Bake a pumpkin pie together.** From rolling out the crust to adding the whipped cream on top, it's a cozy way to embrace the season's flavors, that's easy as pie!

▪ **Start a gratitude list together.** Write down things you're grateful for on slips of paper to create a gratitude jar or tree. Alternatively, you can create a running list to revisit and expand on throughout the year. It makes for a warm evening as you reflect on all your blessings together.

▪ **Go leaf peeping.** The changing leaves of autumn happens faster than you realize, which is why "leaf peeping" makes a perfect seasonal date. Take a scenic drive or hike into a forest or woodlands (typically, mid-October is prime leaf-peeping season) to soak up the vibrant fall foliage.

SEASONAL IDEAS

▪ **Create a seasonal or holiday wreath together.** Use natural materials like pinecones and greenery or add playful touches like ornaments or even small figurines. It will be a daily reminder of your festive date night every time you walk through the door!

▪ **Create your own advent calendar.** Count down to the holidays by making a personalized advent calendar filled with small rewards. Include notes, treats, or activities for each day to help build anticipation not only for the holiday itself but also for daily time connecting together!

▪ **Create your own couples Christmas card.** Celebrate the season by staging a holiday-themed photo shoot for your own couples Christmas card. Whether you go classic, cozy, or funny, dressing up and posing for photos adds a festive flair to your holidays.

▪ **Bake Christmas cookies.** Get into the holiday spirit with a cookie-baking date. Try traditional favorites or experiment with new recipes, and don't forget the icing and sprinkles for decorating!

▪ **Decorate gingerbread houses.** Buy a kit or make your own using icing, candies, and sprinkles to construct a holiday masterpiece. You can even let family and friends vote on whose house wins!

▪ **Go to a Christmas tree farm.** Enjoy wandering through rows of evergreens, take in the scent of pine, and maybe even warm up with hot chocolate afterward for a cozy and memorable way to kick off the holiday season.

▪ **Decorate the Christmas tree together.** Gather your ornaments, lights, and tinsel, and decorate a Christmas tree together. Playing holiday music, wear festive sweaters, and maybe even add a new ornament each year.

Create homemade Christmas presents. Whether it's hand-painted ornaments, baked goods, or making memorable keepsakes, crafting together can be a time of bonding as well as blessing others. Bonus: Your shopping list will also feel a bit more manageable!

Decorate your own holiday wrapping paper. Use stamps, paint, markers, or stencils on plain brown or white paper to create personalized patterns and designs that will add a personal touch to your gift-giving.

Create your own snow globes. Get into the spirit by making your own winter wonderland scenes: Use mason jars, small figurines, glitter, and water to design snowy worlds for a crafty and cozy date night.

Drive around to view holiday lights. Bundle up, hop in the car, and drive around to see houses decked out in lights. Bring along hot cocoa and holiday music to turn it into a festive tour.

Visit an outdoor light installation. Just because the temperatures are dropping doesn't mean you have to stay inside. Many cities put on dazzling outdoor light installations that can be the perfect romantic backdrop for photos, conversation, and walking hand-in-hand together.

See a holiday performance. Embrace the festive spirit by attending a Christmas performance together, like *The Nutcracker* or *A Christmas Carol*. It's a classic way to cozy up and celebrate the most wonderful time of the year.

- **Attend a live nativity scene.** Many churches and community centers host live nativity events that bring the Christmas story to life with real actors, actual animals (which you can often feed), and even live music.

- **Attend a candlelight Christmas Eve service.** Many churches offer candlelight services open to the public, which often include traditional Christmas carols, candles, and a variety of holiday reflections—a perfect way to get into the holiday spirit.

- **Create a mini ball drop at home.** Start by crafting the "ball" using a foam sphere or balloon covered in glitter, sequins, or metallic paper so that when the clock strikes midnight, you can lower (or pop!) it as you ring in the New Year together!

- **Brainstorm New Years' resolutions together.** Start the New Year off right by being intentional about what you want to accomplish in the months ahead. Whether they're individual goals or things you want to achieve together, sharing your goals will bring you closer.

- **Create your own holiday tradition.** Invent a unique tradition just for the two of you! Whether it's an annual dinner recipe, a themed movie marathon, or a quirky holiday game, it's a date that you can look forward to each year, making your holidays feel even more special together.

Long-Distance Ideas

Just because you're physically apart—whether temporarily or for a longer amount of time—doesn't mean you can't connect and share meaningful moments together. With a little creativity and effort, you can turn the distance into an opportunity to grow, no matter the miles between you!

- **Watch a movie or show together.** Video call or text reactions to one another while viewing. Discuss your thoughts afterward, and don't forget the popcorn!

- **Have a dinner date together.** Get the same kind of food and set up a video call so you can eat up together.

- **Cook food together.** Decide on a recipe you both want to make, and work together, virtually, as you simultaneously cook the food together. Then, enjoy the fruits of your labor afterward!

- **Take random photos to document your day.** Help each other feel like they're there with you by taking photos of ordinary moments throughout the day and sharing them with one another.

▨ **Mail a surprise postcard.** Go old-fashioned and send one another a letter or postcard in the mail, sharing your thoughts about each other, hopes for the future, or just what you've been up to recently.

▨ **Have a virtual tasting together.** Go to the same store and pick out the same kind of food or drink. Then, do a tasting together while you video chat!

▨ **Play online or video games together.** Find games that you can play together virtually as a way to connect and have fun at the same time!

▨ **Host your own book club together.** Pick a book and take turns reading chapters aloud to each other over the phone or read it individually before discussing together.

▨ **Stargaze together at night.** Take time to marvel at the night sky together. Try to find the same constellation (you can use an app like SkyView) so that you're both looking at it at the same time! Maybe you can even spot a shooting star and make a wish together!

▨ **Exchange gifts.** If you're apart for a holiday or special event, coordinate to send gifts to one another in advance. Then, wait and open them simultaneously during a video chat as you celebrate together!

▨ **Take an online class or webinar together.** Explore a new hobby or learn more about a topic of interest to both of you by taking a virtual class (or even watching YouTube videos) together. It could be arts, a lecture about a topic you both are interested in, or even do a workout together!

LONG-DISTANCE IDEAS

▪ **Plan a trip together.** Use this time apart to plan your next trip, vacation or visit together. Discuss your travel ideas and research places to help build the anticipation of your next journey together!

▪ **Build a songs playlist.** Create a shared playlist where you can both add songs. It can be songs that remind you of each other or of your favorite memories or simply songs that you like. But either way, they'll help you connect as you listen to them throughout your day.

Planning Tips

Let's face it—while the idea of regular date nights sounds amazing, the reality is that life often gets in the way.

Between work commitments, parenting duties, tight budgets, and unexpected obstacles, finding time to connect with your partner can feel like an uphill battle. But here's the good news: With a little creativity and planning, it's possible to prioritize quality time together, no matter what challenges you face.

This section is dedicated to helping couples navigate the most common barriers to date nights. From busy schedules and financial constraints to finding childcare, we'll explore practical solutions that make regular date nights accessible and enjoyable for everyone.

That's because even in the face of constraints, date nights remain an invaluable way to nurture your relationship. In the following pages, you'll find tips and ideas tailored to help you overcome a variety of challenges as you rediscover the joy of spending meaningful time together. Because no matter how hectic or complicated life gets, your relationship is worth it.

WHEN YOU HAVE TIME CONSTRAINTS

Put date nights on the calendar: Treat dates like any other important appointment and block the time off in both partners' calendars. This will help you make sure they happen and you reap the rewards of regular date nights.

Plan mini dates: You've heard someone say that the best workout is the one that you actually do? The same is true when it comes to date nights. They don't have to be long or extravagant. If your schedule is busy, opt for shorter dates like a 30-minute coffee break or a walk together during lunch. Something is always better than nothing!

Consider alternative times: Turn non-traditional hours, like first thing in the morning or late at night when the rest of the family is tucked into bed, into quality time. Or consider taking a vacation day off work and planning your date during daytime hours when places are less crowded or the kids are still in school.

WHEN YOU HAVE KIDS

Get creative with babysitters: Consider enlisting trusted relatives or coordinating babysitting exchanges with other parents to free you up to make date nights happen. Many local churches, daycares or community centers also offer affordable "parents night out" services where you can drop your kids off with licensed caregivers for an evening to yourselves.

Plan an at-home date night: If childcare is an issue, consider planning at an-home date night, whether it's letting the kids watch a movie while you and your partner connect or waiting until they're tucked into bed to spend one-on-one time together. Just plan accordingly and take a nap ahead of time if you need to!

WHEN BUDGET IS AN ISSUE

Prioritize time over money: Remember that the experience together is what matters most—sometimes, simply sitting outside to stargaze together can be more meaningful than the fanciest restaurant meal. Lots of the ideas featured in this book are completely free and priceless when it comes to the memories made!

Put it in the budget: Make your date night a line-item in your budget, and get creative about how to use that money. Maybe you purchase take-out while streaming a movie at home. Or eat dinner before hitting a comedy club. Allowing yourselves to splurge every once and awhile will help date nights continue to feel special.

Research free and discount attractions: Many area newspapers feature calendars of events listing free attractions, or use apps like Groupon or local deal websites to enjoy activities without breaking the bank. In addition, museums and national parks also occasionally offer admission-free days that you can use to plan your next date night accordingly.

WHEN LIFE IS STRESSFUL

Treat date nights like an oasis. When life is hard—whether because of health issues, tension at work, or family dynamics—date night should be part of your self-care routine. Rather than feel the burden of having to plan an elaborate date, perhaps set realistic expectations and choose accessible activities that you find relaxing and rejuvenating.

Rotate planning responsibilities. Share the workload by alternating who organizes the date night. Not only will this protect one partner from shouldering too much of the burden, it also will ensure that that you each get to pick date-night activities that appeal to your preferences.

By identifying potential obstacles and employing creative strategies, you can prioritize meaningful date nights, no matter the challenges you face. Whether it's finding time in a packed schedule, sticking to a budget, or working around family responsibilities, creative solutions will ensure that no excuse will ever come between you and your next date night again!

Conversation Starters

Okay, you're on your date night. Now what?! Sometimes it can be hard to break out of routine conversations, finding ourselves taking about the same old things—work, kids, finances—even when we get to go on a date night.

That's why we've brainstormed 50 thought-provoking conversation starters that you can use to jumpstart your date, whether you pick one to discuss on the drive to your destination, while waiting for your dinner to be served, or at any point when there's a lull.

However you use them, they're insightful inquiries that are sure to spark deep discussions!

1. What did you want to be when you were a child?

2. What's something you've learned about yourself recently?

3. If we won the lottery tomorrow, what's the first thing you'd do?

4. What's the weirdest food you've ever tried or want to try in the future?

5. What's your favorite memory involving the outdoors?
6. Which meal do you look forward to the most?
7. Who is someone that inspires you and that you'd like to be more like?
8. What's a memory of us that always makes you smile?
9. What in your life are you the most proud of?
10. What's the most adventurous thing we've done together so far?
11. If we could relive one day from our relationship, which would it be?
12. How has our relationship changed you in a positive way?
13. If you could instantly master any skill, what would it be and why?
14. What's a quirky habit I have that you secretly like?
15. What's your biggest dream for us as a couple?
16. If you could give your younger self one piece of advice, what would it be?
17. What do I do that lets you know that I love you?
18. What would be your ideal day together if time and money weren't a factor?
19. What's one thing you wish people understood about you?

DATE NIGHT CONVERSATION STARTERS

20. If you could design your dream house, what's one must-have feature?

21. How do you usually process conflict, and how can I support you better during disagreements?

22. What's your dream destination, and what would you want to do there?

23. What's one bucket list item we should check off together as a couple?

24. What's your all-time favorite movie and why?

25. If you could only eat one type of cuisine for a year, what would it be?

26. Do you have a reoccurring dream or nightmare?

27. What was your favorite holiday tradition when you were a child?

28. If you could visit any natural wonder, where would you go?

29. What's the most creative thing you've ever done?

30. What's a dream or goal you've kept to yourself but would love to pursue?

31. What's a small gesture I could do more often that would mean a lot to you?

32. What's one thing you learned from your family that you want to keep in our relationship?

33. What's a mistake you made in the past that taught you an important lesson?

34. What's something you've been too afraid to try but secretly want to?
35. What emotion do you think comes to you most naturally? Which one do you think you struggle the most to express?
36. What's your least favorite routine task or household chore? What's your favorite?
37. What was a time when you got in trouble as a kid?
38. What would be the most enjoyable way for you to spend $100?
39. What's a talent you wish you had?
40. What do you think you worry about the most?
41. If you had an heirloom to pass down, what would it be?
42. Do you remember what you first thought of me when we met?
43. What's a part of yourself you're still learning to accept?
44. What is your favorite thing to do on vacation?
45. What do you think is the most important element of a healthy relationship?
46. What is a favorite or memorable scent?
47. How do you calm down when you're feeling overwhelmed?
48. What's your favorite way to spend time outside?

49. What is one thing that it seems like everyone else loves that you hate?

50. What are three adjectives you'd use to describe yourself? What three adjectives would you use to describe me?

Are you having FUN yet?!

Leave a review
and tell us what you think!

They really help!

Your Turn!

Use the following pages to list out your favorite date-night ideas, add your own, or track the new dates you try.

www.ingramcontent.com/pod-product-compliance
Lightning Source LLC
Chambersburg PA
CBHW070524030426
42337CB00016B/2089